At a Glance Series

DVD and Lesson Book

DVD Guitar Technique

Written by Brad McLemore, Chad Johnson & Michael Mueller
Video Performers: Doug Boduch, Troy Stetina & Marcus Henderson

ISBN: 978-1-4234-6222-4

HAL•LEONARD®
CORPORATION
7777 W. BLUEMOUND RD. P.O. BOX 13819 MILWAUKEE, WI 53213

Visit Hal Leonard Online at
www.halleonard.com

Table of Contents

Introduction

Welcome to *DVD Guitar Technique*, from Hal Leonard's At a Glance series. Technique is an important part of every guitar player's development and advancement. More than just learning to play fast, it's a quest to leave you without limitations. While scales and patterns are a great way to build speed and dexterity, playing actual songs can be a more musical way to reach the same technical goals. This book will provide you with a little of both. Just remember, everyone develops at a different pace, and through regular practice and dedication, you'll be surprised by what you can do! So let's dig in and do some wood shedding!

WARMING UP

In this chapter, we're going to look at all kinds of stretches and warm-up exercises. These are not specific to any style or playing level. They're designed to target the specific muscle groups commonly used in playing the guitar. Guitarists are notorious for not properly warming up before a practice or performance. This not only prevents us from reaching peak performance, it also increases the risk of serious injuries, such as tendonitis.

Stretching

Playing guitar is a physical activity, and we need to warm up our muscles the same way athletes do. Devoting a little time to this before you start playing will help you make the most of your time on the instrument. So let's start with a few simple stretches that will cover just about all the muscles we use while playing the guitar. Try to remain relaxed as you warm up and always remember to breathe, even when you are holding a stretched position.

Fingers & Forearms

Pointing Up

For the first stretch, just reach out with your right hand in front of you as if you are making a "stop" gesture.

Then, with your left hand, gently pull your fingertips toward you. You will feel the muscles in your forearm and fingers stretching. Don't overdo it! You should not stretch to the point of pain. Hold this position for about 15 seconds, then switch hands and repeat the exercise.

Pointing Down

The second stretch is the opposite of the first one. Instead of pointing your fingers up, point them down toward the floor. Place your left hand on the outside of your right hand and gently pull the back of your right hand toward you. This stretch will target the other side of your forearm. Once again hold this position for 15 seconds, then switch hands and repeat.

Triceps & Back

You'll need to stand up for these next few stretches.

Clasp your hands together in front of your waist.

With your hands remaining clasped, reach straight up as high as you can with your hands over your head. Hold your hands stretched above your head for about 20 seconds. This stretch will focus on loosening your triceps and back.

Biceps & Chest

Our next stretch will focus on your biceps and chest.

First, clutch your hands behind your back.

Slowly reach back as far as you can, trying to create a right angle between your arms and back. Hold this position for about 20 seconds.

All Throughout

For the fifth stretch, you'll need a wall or something sturdy to lean against.

With your feet shoulder-width apart and the wall to your side, reach out and place your hand against the wall, letting the wall support your weight.

With your back straight and your weight against the wall, turn your head and focus on something in the opposite direction. Hold this position for about 15 seconds. Shake out your arm, and then repeat the exercise with the other arm. You'll feel this stretch all throughout your body, from your hand down to your hip.

Now that you've loosened up the major muscle groups involved in playing the guitar, you're ready to pick up your guitar and perform some specific warm-up exercises.

Exercises

We're going to start with a few chromatic-based exercises that will work both of our hands.

Exercise 1

1–2–3–4

This first warm up exercise is based on the classic 1–2–3–4 exercise you may have learned when you first began to play the guitar. We've created a slight twist, however. Each time you move to a new string, you will start on the next finger but continue through the 1–2–3–4 pattern.

In other words, begin on the sixth string in eighth position playing fingers 1–2–3–4. Next, go to the fifth string and play 2–3–4–1. On the fourth string, play 3–4–1–2, and finally on the third string play 4–1–2–3. On the second string, you're back to 1–2–3–4. Continue on the first string playing 2–3–4–1. Shift down one fret to the next position and keep the pattern going by remaining on the first string and playing 3–4–1–2. On the second string, play 4–1–2–3, and so on. Once you play the four notes on the sixth string, you're ready to shift down one more fret and begin the pattern all over again in sixth position.

It sounds a bit complicated, but be sure to check out the DVD. Once you try it, it will become clear. If you follow the directions given, you'll work your way down the fretboard from the eighth position to the first position. For a somewhat shorter warm-up, you might try starting in the sixth or fourth position. Make sure you're alternate picking throughout: down-up-down-up. Remember that you are still warming up, so play slowly and cleanly.

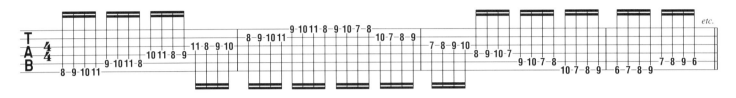

After you've done this, repeat the same exercise using hammer-ons and pull-offs. With this exercise, you will only pluck each string once. This is a difficult exercise, so take it slowly and stop and take a break if you need to.

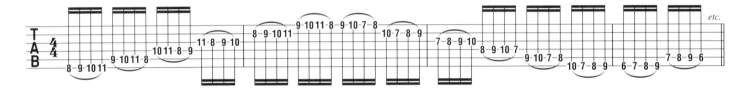

Exercise 2

4–3–2–1

The second exercise is simply the opposite of Exercise 1. We will be descending through the finger pattern: 4–3–2–1, 3–2–1–4, 2–1–4–3, 1–4–3–2, 4–3–2–1, etc. Once again, continue the pattern all the way to the first position.

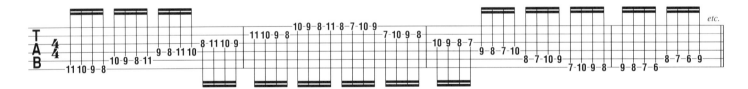

Once you've completed exercise 2, try the same thing using pull-offs and hammer-ons.

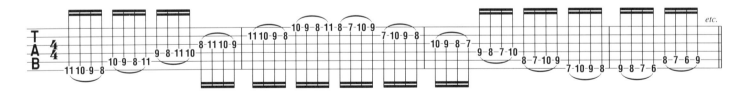

Exercise 3

1–2–3

For the next exercise, we're going to use a variation of the previous exercises and use only three notes per string. Once again, you will use alternate picking throughout, allowing you to practice both methods used when crossing strings with the pick: inside and outside the strings. In other words, the first note of each string will have a different pick direction. You will pluck the sixth string down-up-down, the fifth string, up-down-up, etc.

You can play these with either your first, second, and third fingers, or use your second, third, and fourth to really work out your pinky!

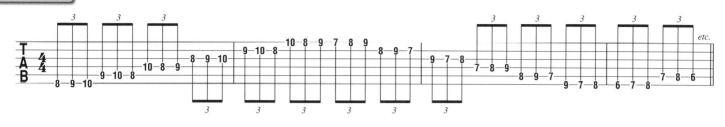

Continue this pattern all the way down to the first fret. Next, again do the same thing with legato technique.

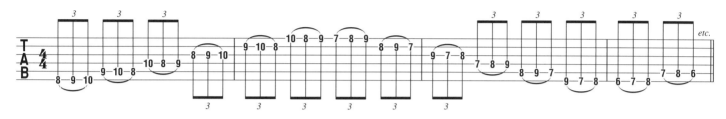

Exercise 4

3–2–1

Exercise 4 is the opposite of Exercise 3. We will be descending through the finger pattern: 3–2–1, 2–1–3, 1–3–2, etc.

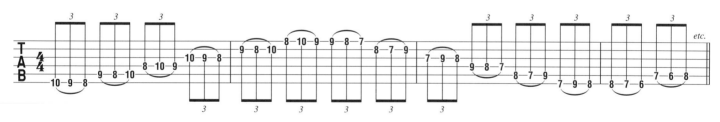

Work down to the first fret, and then play the same thing legato.

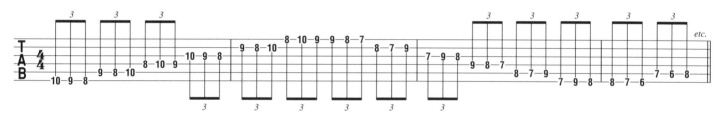

Exercise 5

1–2–3–4 on Different Strings

Exercise 5 concentrates on picking four consecutive strings. Use alternate picking throughout so that you get the ultimate picking warm up. You will use the same 1–2–3–4 finger pattern, except each finger will be on a different string.

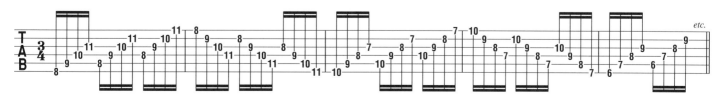

Again, continue to move the sequence all the way down the neck.

Chord Reach Stretch

The last warm up exercise is a stretching exercise for your left hand. It sounds a little ugly, but it will help increase your chord reach.

We're going to start in the eighth position again with one finger per fret, but this time we'll be playing "chords" with each finger on a different string. Start with your first finger on the sixth string, second finger on the fifth string, third finger on the fourth string, and fourth finger on the third string. Play one string at a time from low to high, allowing all the notes to ring together. Then move all of your fingers down one string and play the fifth, fourth, third, and second strings. Move your fingers down one more time and play the fourth, third, second, and first strings.

Next, we'll reverse the shape and start with your first finger on the first string, second finger on the second string, third finger on the third string, and fourth finger on the fourth string, again playing notes from low to high. Next, move your fingers up one string and play the fifth, fourth, third, and second strings. Finally, move them down one more time and play the sixth, fifth, fourth, and third strings.

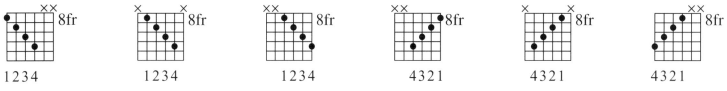

We've just completed the first part of the exercise. Next, move your first finger back one fret, creating a stretch between your first and second finger. Then move back up and down through the pattern.

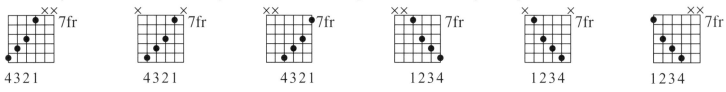

Next, move your second finger back one fret to create a stretch between your second and third fingers. Once again, move back up and down through the pattern.

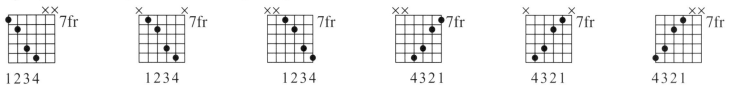

Finally, move your third finger back one fret to create a stretch between your third and fourth finger. Move up and down through pattern.

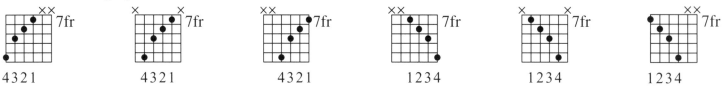

Move your fourth finger back one fret, and you're back where you started, but one fret lower in the seventh position.

Continue this sequence down the fretboard until you can't stretch anymore. You can start this exercise in any position. Obviously, the closer you get to the first position, the greater the stretch, so be sure to start higher on the fretboard.

Well that's the end of a pretty extensive warm up. By this point, you should be stretched out, limber, and ready to go. Try to make these warm up exercises part of your daily routine. You'll increase your control and dexterity, and you'll be less likely to suffer injury while playing.

ALTERNATE PICKING

Alternate picking is a very efficient technique for producing clean and even-sounding notes with a pick. In this chapter, we'll look closely at the technique and give you some exercises for developing it.

 Alternate picking means that your pick strikes the string from two directions: down and up. First, we'll look at the downstroke, which is when you strike the string from above, down toward the floor. It's indicated by the rectangular mark on the tab. When we strike the string from below, up toward the ceiling, it's called an upstroke and is indicated by the V-shaped mark. Below is an example of both the upstroke and the downstroke written in tab.

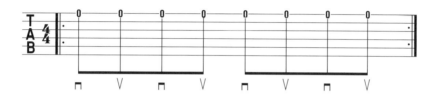

As you practice alternate picking, it's always a good idea to use a metronome and tap your foot with the beat. Let's start with the musical example above, which simply uses the open first string. The downstrokes happen along with the click of the metronome as your foot taps the floor. The upstrokes happen when your foot comes up off the floor. In other words, your pick will go down and strike the string at the same time your foot hits the floor. Your pick will then go up and strike the string at the same time your foot reaches its highest point.

 Although it is common to place downstrokes on downbeats, it's also important to practice playing upstrokes on downbeats, as certain licks or phrases may lay out better either way, depending on the string group. Keep your foot tapping the same as before, but this time play the upstroke when your foot hits the ground and the downstroke when your foot reaches its highest point.

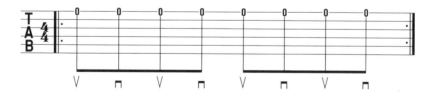

The basic alternate picking motion should come from the wrist. We want to strive for the same relaxed movement in single-note alternate picking as when strumming chords. The only difference is that the hand is closer to the strings and uses a much smaller range of motion. To help it glide through the string in either direction without getting stuck, the pick should be held at a slight angle to the string.

Some players think the upward angle allows for faster alternate picking, but it doesn't work well for incorporating other picking techniques such as sweep-picking or hybrid-picking (playing with both and pick and fingers). I recommend you start with the downward angle and, after you've mastered that, try the upward angle. Holding the pick between the thumb and first finger, try curling the other fingers up keeping them out of the way. Be careful not to clinch your fist with tension; instead, you want to keep your right hand relaxed as you pick.

Before you work on other picking techniques like sweep or economy picking, it's important to extensively practice alternate picking. Whether you're repeating notes on one string, or moving from string to string within a scale or arpeggio, alternating strictly is an important technique to master. It will not only speed up your picking hand, but will also teach you to synchronize the two hands with solid timing. While the first four exercises and excerpts are geared for mainly the pick hand, the last three will strengthen the timing between both hands.

Down-Up or Up-Down

Let's start with a simple exercise using open strings. Begin on the sixth string and pick eighth notes starting with a downstroke. The down stroke will be on the beat, and the upstroke will come on the upbeat. Then play the example using the opposite picking motion: upstrokes on the beat, and downstrokes on the upbeat. Be sure to use a metronome for solid timing and to measure your progress and speed. Play this exercise on all six strings.

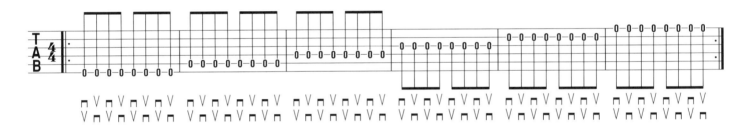

The example below from the Scorpion's hit "Rock You Like a Hurricane" uses a pattern based on sixteenth notes. While this is played primarily on a single note, it's a great exercise for alternate picking since the rhythm breaks out of a straight sixteenth-note pattern, incorporating eighth notes as well. Even though you don't pick every sixteenth note, you want to keep the motion of your picking hand moving as if you are striking every sixteenth note. For beats 2 and 3 of the first three measures, pick down-down-up-up-down to keep your right hand picking motion consistent. For beats 2 and 3 of the last measure, pick down-down-up-down-down-up.

Words and Music by Herman Rarebell,
Klaus Meine and Rudolf Schenker

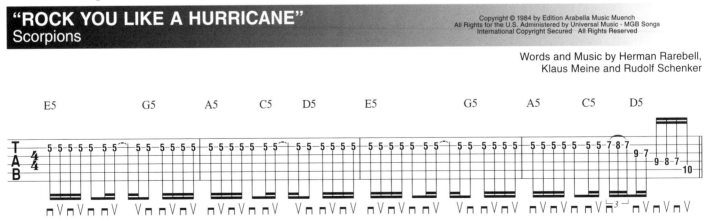

Double-Picking Notes

A good exercise to strengthen your alternate picking is to play a familiar scale and pick each note in the scale twice while alternating the down and upstrokes. The example below uses the familiar A minor pentatonic scale. Remember to also play the same exercise starting with the upstroke.

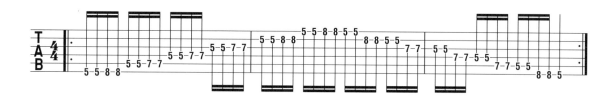

Another excerpt from "Rock You Like A Hurricane" shows how this simple climb up the E minor pentatonic scale can create excitement in a solo. Notice how this lick builds by double-picking up the scale to pinched harmonic bends on the first and second strings and ends with a classic run down the scale to the tonic on the fourth string. Be sure to use a slight palm mute on the lower strings until you get to the position shift for the last two beats of the first full measure.

"ROCK YOU LIKE A HURRICANE"
Scorpions

Words and Music by Herman Rarebell,
Klaus Meine and Rudolf Schenker

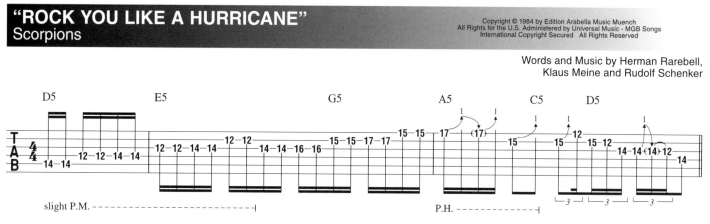

Tremolo Picking

Tremolo picking is the technique of picking a single note as fast as possible. Most tremolo licks involve changing notes in a rhythmic manner on the same string while picking as fast as possible. A good exercise to develop this is to play a scale on one string while applying the tremolo technique.

Here's an exercise to get started.

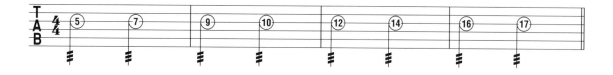

A famous example of this technique is used in Eddie Van Halen's guitar masterpiece "Eruption." Eddie starts by tremolo picking a simple E major scale melody. He then adds some embellishments as he moves all the way down the first string. Even though you're adding slides, continue picking as fast as possible to drive home the tremolo effect.

"ERUPTION"
Van Halen

Music by David Lee Roth, Edward Van Halen,
Alex Van Halen and Michael Anthony

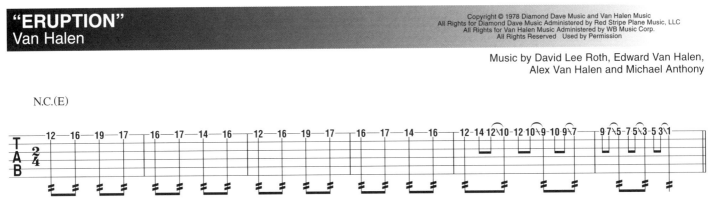

The next group of exercises are geared toward helping develop the coordination between your picking hand and your fretting hand. These exercises use all four fingers on the fretting hand. Try to press each finger down on the string just when the pick strikes it.

Four Notes Per String

This is the old 1–2–3–4 exercise, similar to the one we used in the warm up section. Here, though, you should be warmed up, so you can increase the speed of this exercise until you're no longer able to play it cleanly. Be sure to tap your foot on the floor as you play each downstroke. Also be aware that if you start the pattern with a downstroke, each time you change strings you will be using a down as well. It's also a good idea to start the whole pattern with an upstroke. This will strengthen the coordination of the two hands even further.

Once you've completed the pattern across the neck, keep playing the pattern by moving up one fret and coming back across the neck to the sixth string. Continue up the fretboard until you reach fret 12.

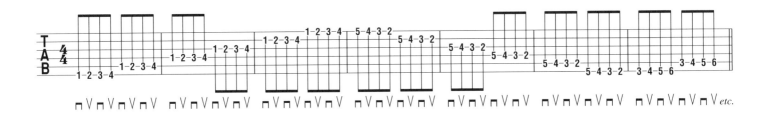

Three Notes Per String

Now let's try three notes per string with the F major scale. Since we're using an odd number of notes on each string, the first note of each new string will begin with a different picking direction.

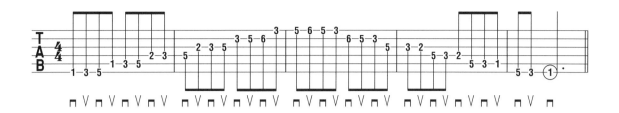

In the solo from "Heaven Tonight," Yngwie Malmsteen finishes with a blazing run up the E mixolydian scale starting on the 3rd (G♯) and then back down adding a ♭9th. This not only adds some chromatic tension, but it also keeps the three-notes-per-string pattern consistent.

"HEAVEN TONIGHT"
Yngwie Malmsteen

Words and Music by Yngwie Malmsteen
and Joe Lynn Turner

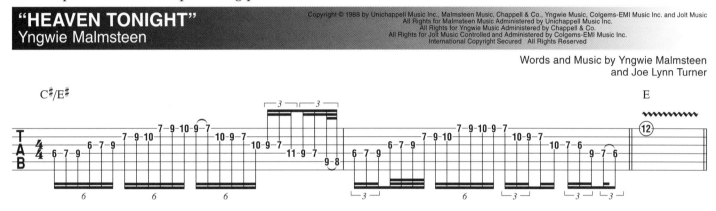

Two Notes Per String

Finally, we'll apply the alternate picking technique to two notes per string using the F minor pentatonic scale. You can practice this with any scale or arpeggio that uses two notes per string, but of coarse the most common scale pattern is the pentatonic scale.

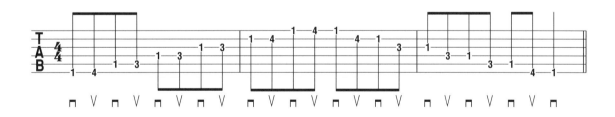

And here's a little example lick using the scale that you might hear Eric Johnson do.

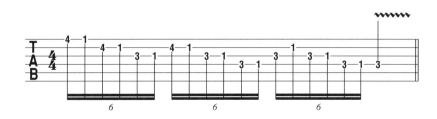

Speaking of Eric, in this excerpt from "Zenland," Johnson takes the E♭ minor pentatonic scale, with an F (9th) added for color, and explores some two-note-per-string patterns. Note the position shift midway through the measure that incorporates the F in place of the G♭ (♭3rd). Practice this lick with and without the slurs for a great alternate picking workout.

"ZENLAND"
Eric Johnson

By Eric Johnson

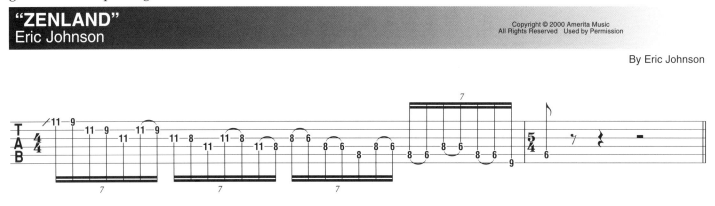

Accents and Hemiola

It's a good idea to apply some accents while practicing alternate picking. Otherwise, you may be limiting yourself to only accenting the downbeat or downstrokes within a pattern. A common and interesting way to add syncopation is to use accents to create what is called a *hemiola* effect. We'll start with a pattern that uses all eighth notes on the note A at the fifth fret of the first string. Accent the first eighth note and then accent every fourth note after that. Once you've completed three measures of eighth notes, the accent will end up back on the downbeat of the measure.

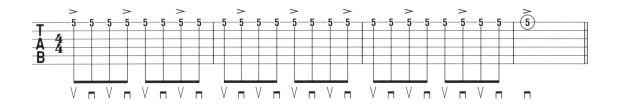

We can also apply the hemiola effect to a scale. Let's play the A natural minor scale pattern starting on the sixth string, fifth fret. Be sure to use strict alternate picking while accenting every fourth note. You will then notice that the accent will also alternate between the upstroke and downstroke.

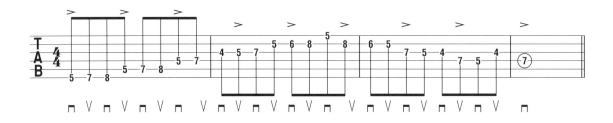

14

The outro riff of Mr. Big's "Addicted to That Rush" has a repetitive pattern that creates the hemiola affect. While this example uses slurs (hammer-ons), you can try picking each note for a great accent exercise. Notice how the hemiola affect is broken at the end of the second measure and fourth measures to create a two-measure phrase, which is then repeated for measures 3–4. Measures 5–8, however, maintain the 3-against-4 hemiola throughout.

Words and Music by Paul Gilbert,
William Sheehan and Pat Torpey

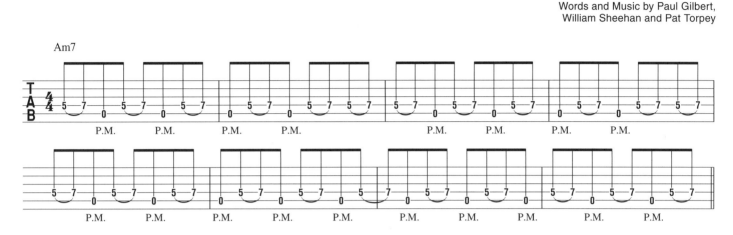

Got Tension? Relax!

In order to improve technique and develop finger independence, speed, and dexterity, you will need to dedicate yourself to some repetitive practice time. It is extremely important to remain relaxed as you work on these skills. It's not uncommon for musicians to unconsciously become tense the faster or harder they play. But realize that tension in your fingers, arms, back, or anywhere for that matter will only get in the way of you achieving your maximum performance. Therefore, check yourself for tension often as part of your practice routine. If you feel tension, try these short exercises and relax between each short burst.

These short examples should be played at a comfortable speed to begin with. Use the rests to take a breath and consciously relax your whole body. As you increase the speed, be sure to not increase tension anywhere; in fact, try to become even more relaxed as you speed up.

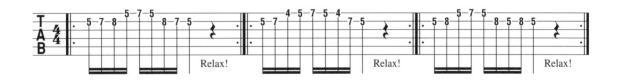

This three-measure example from Night Ranger's "Don't Tell Me You Love Me" is an example of the short speed burst followed by a long note. The long notes with vibrato should be your chance to focus on relaxing your picking hand and relieving any tension before the next quick sixteenth-note run. You can follow this example and make up your own exercise or solo. Pick a series of target notes, and then play a series of quick notes that lead to the target note. Experiment with various scales, but most of all remember to RELAX!

"DON'T TELL ME YOU LOVE ME"
Night Ranger

Words and Music by
Jack Blades

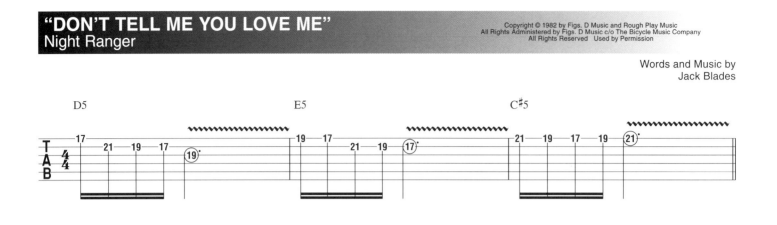

Muting

It is important to practice the technique exercises with all of the sounds you might use in a performance. Playing with a distorted guitar sound versus a clean sound can present specific challenges. For instance, when playing with a distorted electric sound, you will want to use your picking hand to use a bit of palm muting so that the notes are clear and unwanted strings don't ring. Be aware that both hands need to mute strings that are not supposed to sound, but you will use your pick hand to create the deliberate sound known as *palm muting*.

Here's how the four-note-per-string exercise looks when played with palm muting.

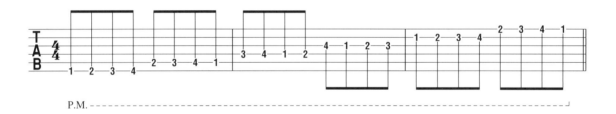

This four-measure riff using the F# harmonic minor scale from Yngwie Malmsteen's "Far Beyond the Sun" is a great scalar example of applying the palm mute. Beginning on the fifth string with your pinky, the lick climbs to the sixth note of the scale and then returns to the root. The first and third measures include a sixteenth-note triplet at the peak of the phrase for added flash. Note how the ending climb releases the palm mute beginning on beat 3 of the fourth measure.

"FAR BEYOND THE SUN"
Yngwie Malmsteen

By Yngwie Malmsteen

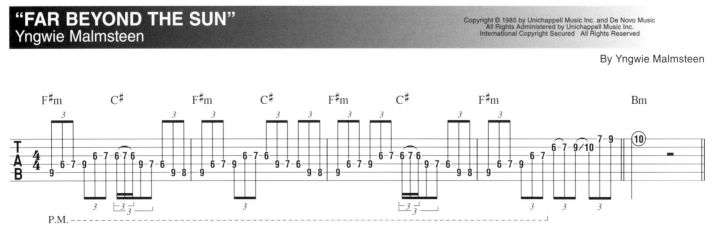

It's a good idea to backtrack and try some of the previous exercises using palm muting to develop the technique. You can also mix in palm muting as a texture. Remember, you don't have to completely go one way or the other. Try playing four notes muted and four notes un-muted throughout one of the warm-up exercises or later in the next chapter on scale sequences.

Picking Mechanics

Let's look closely at the four picking mechanics used when moving from string to string. The first two are examples of leading to a new string with an upstroke, and the third example leads to a new string with a downstroke. Exercise 4 then combines leading to a new string with an upstroke and a downstroke.

Leading with an Upstroke

Although this exercise begins with a downstroke, as you move to a lower sounding string, you will use an upstroke to keep the strict alternation of down and upstrokes. This pattern moves all the way across the neck through the E minor pentatonic scale. Note that leading to a new string with an upstroke occurs any time you play a pattern that has an odd number of notes on a higher string and then moves to a lower string. First, try the first four notes of the pattern to get a feel for the string change leading with the upstroke. Then try the pattern all the way across the neck.

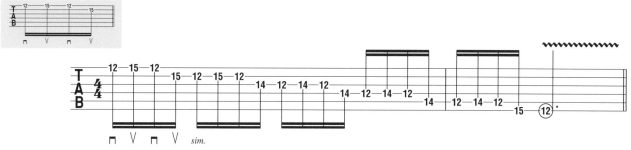

Leading to a higher sounding string with an upstroke is basically the same as the previous technique only going the other direction across the fretboard. The same rule of using any scale or pattern that uses an odd number of notes per string will work. The second example below starts at the bottom of the pentatonic scale and works its way up the scale while using an upstroke on the first note of each new string.

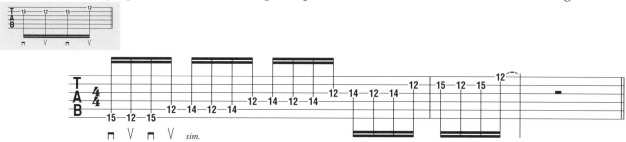

Leading with a Downstroke

Next, we'll lead to a new string with a downstroke. As you've probably figured out already, to accomplish this we'll need a scale or pattern that uses an even number of notes played on each string before moving up or down to the next string. A simple example of this is a pentatonic scale with two notes per string. In this example, we'll play two notes on the first string and then four notes on the second through fifth strings, ending with two notes on the sixth string.

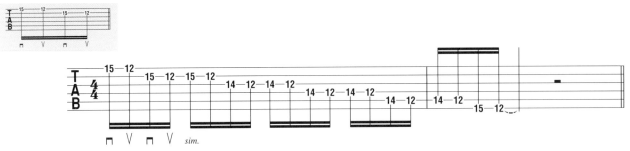

Our final example is a combination of the previous examples. When we move to a new lower sounding string, we'll lead with a downstroke. When we move back to a higher sounding string, we'll use an upstroke. Again, be sure to use strict alternate picking throughout the pattern.

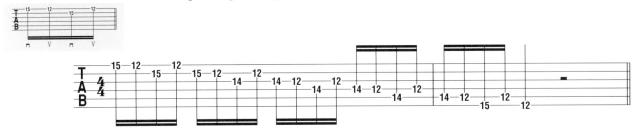

The only way to get good at alternate picking is to practice it. You can use any scales, arpeggios, or sequences you know to help develop the technique. Remember to always use a metronome and track your tempos with a written log. This will allow you to document your progress and set goals for yourself.

Here's a short classical-type exercise that uses arpeggios on the top strings. Be sure to alternate pick throughout, and remember to stay relaxed and tap your foot along with the beat.

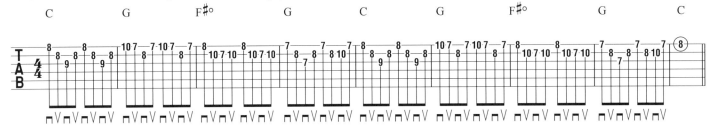

It's a good idea to practice alternate picking while developing your memorization and reading skills. Just about any instrument written in the treble clef will work. Classical violin and clarinet studies or etudes are especially good for guitar. Many guitarists use Paganini's "24 Caprices" or "Moto Perpetuo" because they include long passages of continuous notes. Another good source for alternate picking is bluegrass fiddle tunes.

In this four-measure excerpt from Niccolò Paganini's "Caprice in A minor, No. 24," you can see a challenging exercise that outlines A minor and E major chords. This is also a great example for practicing position shifts, since each measure involves at least two separate positions.

"CAPRICE #24 op. 1"
Niccolà Paganini

By Niccolo Paganini

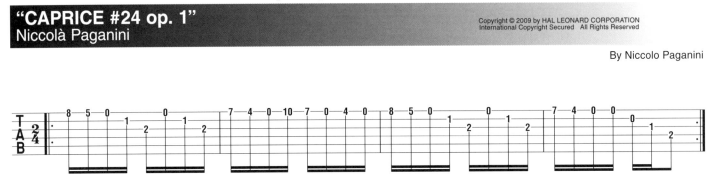

SCALE SEQUENCES

Most aspiring lead guitarists begin their quest for fretboard mastery by learning scale patterns played straight up and down scales. While that's important for hand coordination and finger dexterity, it can make for a pretty dull solo. In this chapter, we're going to learn how to use scale sequences to improve your chops and add excitement and variety to your solos.

So what is a scale sequence? It's simply a series of notes played in a specific numerical or intervallic pattern throughout a particular scale. For example, you can create scale sequences using three-, four-, five-, or even six-note patterns. Or, you can create a scale sequence using 3rd or 4th intervals. In this chapter, we will do all of the above.

Three-Note Pentatonic Patterns

We'll start using the box shape of a B minor pentatonic scale that is familiar to most guitarists. This first pattern uses a three-note sequence played through the B minor pentatonic scale form. Simply play three notes up the scale, go back down one note, up three notes, down one note, and so on until you work your way through the entire position of the scale.

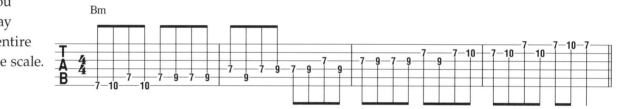

In this excerpt from Carlos Santana's "Song of the Wind," he uses the same three-note pattern sequence going up an A minor pentatonic scale. He adds a few hammer-ons and pull-offs for texture and, while still using groups of three notes, breaks out of strictly playing the sequence once he reaches the first string.

"SONG OF THE WIND"
Carlos Santana

By Gregg Rolie, Neal Schon
and Carlos Santana

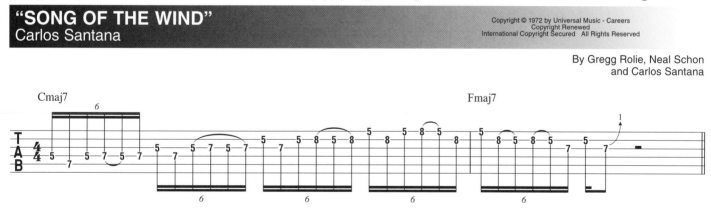

We can also perform the same sequence in a descending pattern. Be sure to play all of the examples going up and down the scale.

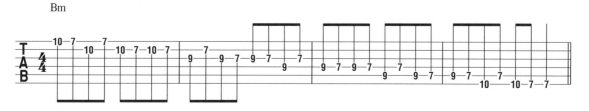

Also in "Song of the Wind," Santana uses the descending version of the sequence for this lick. With the use of various rhythmic groupings and occasionally breaking out of the predictability of the pattern, this is a great example of how to take a sequence and create an interesting lick.

"SONG OF THE WIND"
Carlos Santana

By Gregg Rolie, Neal Schon
and Carlos Santana

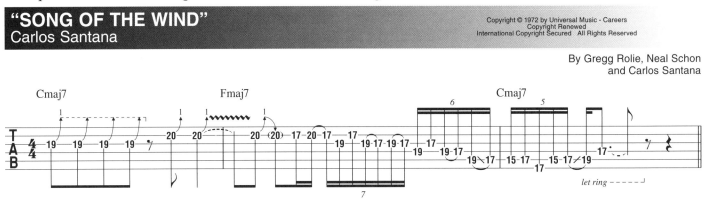

Six-Note Pentatonic Patterns

The next sequence uses a six-note pattern in the B minor pentatonic scale. Since this scale uses two notes on each string, note that each group of six will use three strings and then move back one string to start the next group of six notes.

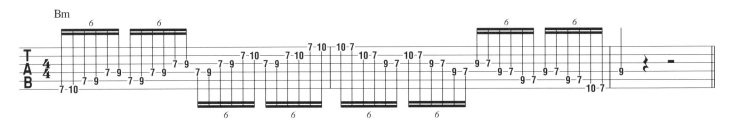

This pattern is a favorite of guitarists like Eric Johnson, Zack Wilde, and Joe Bonamasa. Here's an example of how Eric Johnson incorporates sequencing in the solo of "The Boogie King." As is usually the case with applying the sequence exercises to "real" solos, sticking strictly to a pattern is a little too predictable. Beginning on the second half of beat 4 in the first measure, Johnson begins a six-note sequence similar to our previous exercise. Note how he varies the middle sequence with only five notes and then, after completing the third sequence, he finishes with an octave displacement. Instead of finishing out the G minor pentatonic scale on the sixth string, he jumps to the higher octave G on the fourth string.

"THE BOOGIE KING"
Eric Johnson

By Eric Johnson

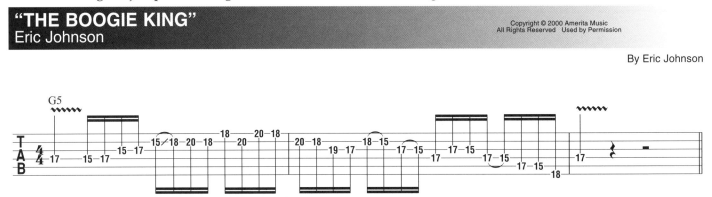

Major and Minor Scale Patterns

The same principles used to sequence pentatonic scales can be used to sequence seven-note major and minor scales. The first example is a descending sequence using triplets throughout the E minor scale.

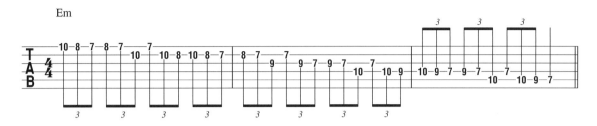

In this excerpt from Yngwie Malmsteen's solo in "I'll See the Light Tonight," Malmsteen uses sequences to ascend the B minor scale beginning and ending on the 2nd, C#. Notice how the lick starts with a sequence on the sixth, fifth, and fourth strings and then breaks the pattern by adding a chromatic G# on the second string, which creates the same sequence on the second and first string.

"I'LL SEE THE LIGHT TONIGHT"
Yngwie Malmsteen

Words and Music by Yngwie Malmsteen
and Jeff Scott Soto

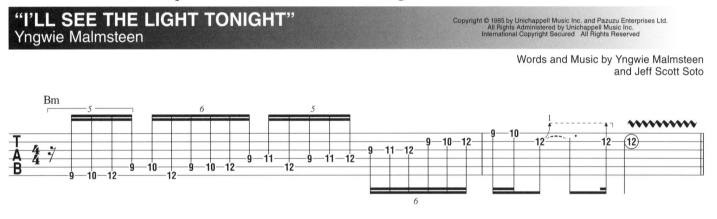

Four-Note Sequences

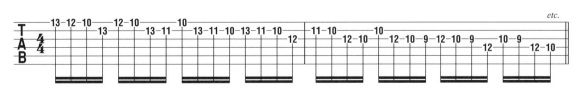

Descending four-note sequences were especially popular with eighties shred guitarists such as Yngwie, Vinnie Moore, and Paul Gilbert. Our first example uses the D natural minor scale starting with F on the first string. Play four notes down the scale, then go back to the E on the first string and play down the scale four more notes. Continue this pattern throughout the scale all the way to the sixth string. Be sure to accent the first note of each four-note sequence.

When employing these types of sequences in a solo, avoid using the entire scale, as it will sound too much like an exercise. Try employing a few sequences in the scale mixed with some other melodic and rhythmic ideas.

Below is an example of how Yngwie mixes in four-note sequences during his solo on "Far Beyond the Sun." The first two measures of this excerpt use various groupings of descending five-, six-, and seven-note runs down the F♯ harmonic minor scale. But the third and fourth measures are dominated by a four-note descending sequence with slight rhythmic variations.

By Yngwie Malmsteen

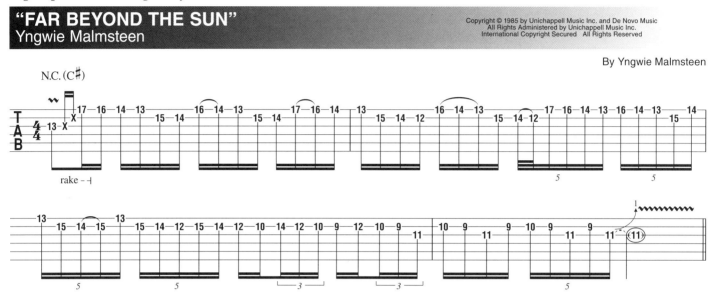

Six–Note Sequences

A six-note sequence makes for a great exercise as well as a phrasing tool. The example below is a fantastic alternate picking chops builder. Top it off with a whole-step bend, and you have a killer crescendo lick to finish your solo. For best phrasing results, accent the first note of each beat in the sequence. You'll find that this type of sequence falls comfortably under your fingers, and you will probably be able to increase the speed fairly quickly. But remember to begin slowly with the accents on the first note of each beat. Also, use strict alternate picking as you gradually increase the speed.

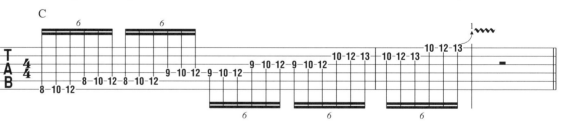

Intervallic Sequences

Intervallic sequences use intervals such as 3rds or 4ths to build a pattern. While you can apply intervallic sequencing to any kind of scale, certain intervals tend to work better with certain scales.

Pentatonic Fourths

A popular intervallic sequence with the pentatonic scale is based on 4ths. This is primarily due to the fact that the scale has the interval of a 4th built into the scale. If you play the minor pentatonic scale and skip every other note, with the exception of the interval between the second and fourth notes of the scale, you will be playing 4th intervals. Try the sequence below that uses the C♯ minor pentatonic.

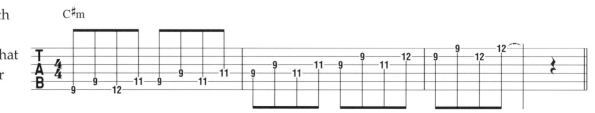

Robben Ford sprinkles the 4th interval throughout the head in the instrumental tune "The Brother." Notice how this excerpt begins with the leap of two consecutive 4ths using the E minor pentatonic scale over the IV chord (A). After using the interval several times as he climbs to the top of the minor pentatonic position, Ford descends an E blues scale, ending on the tonic of the key.

"THE BROTHER" (For Jimmie and Stevie)
Robben Ford

By Robben Ford

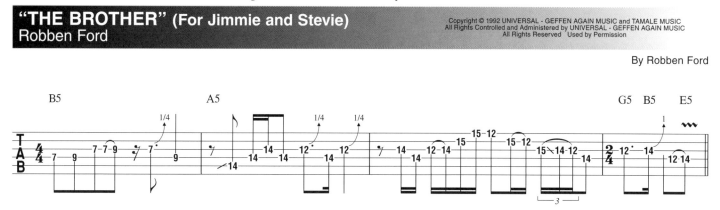

Diatonic 3rds

Major and minor scales lend themselves to using diatonic 3rds to build sequences, since the interval between every other note in the scale is either a major or minor 3rd. We'll use the A major scale for this example beginning on the root. Diatonic 3rds not only build chops, but they sound pretty cool too! You'll immediately recognize their sound.

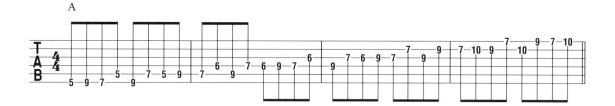

In this two-measure example from Eric Johnson's "Camel's Night Out," Johnson uses diatonic 3rds and 4ths quite frequently as he winds his way down the A Mixolydian scale. This is another good example of building anticipation with repetitive patterns and intervals to pull in the listener while also giving him some resolution by completing the lick on the tonic of the chord (A5).

"CAMEL'S NIGHT OUT"
Eric Johnson

By Kyle Brock
and Mark Younger Smith

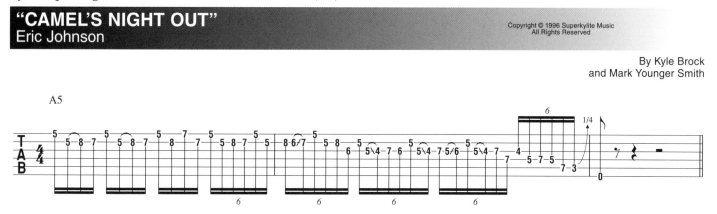

Shifting Positions

So far all of the sequences have been played in one position. But it's also a good idea to practice scale sequences that cover a larger portion of the fretboard. Many guitarists learn scale patterns that go across the neck in one position. The following exercises are a good way to expand your scale/fretboard knowledge by playing scales up and down the neck without being confined to one position. The first example uses the A minor scale on the first string only. We'll start with the root note of the scale at the fifth fret and play a three note sequence shifting up to the next position in the scale for each group of three notes.

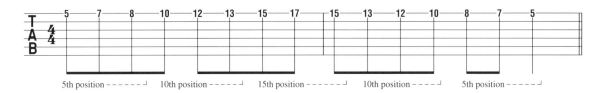

For the next sequence, we'll use a six-note sequence that shifts to a new position for each new group of six. The example below is also in A minor and features a climb from fifth position all the way up to seventeenth position. Note that this type of lick builds valuable musical anticipation along the way.

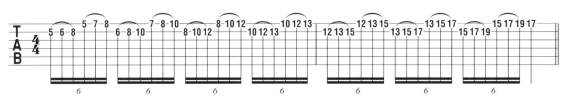

Eric Johnson uses a number of shifts in this excerpt from "Camel's Night Out." He begins the final lick ascending the A major pentatonic scale through various positions. He then finishes the lick entirely in the fourteenth position with a descending sequence down the major pentatonic scale and a few octave jumps.

"CAMEL'S NIGHT OUT"
Eric Johnson

By Kyle Brock
and Mark Younger Smith

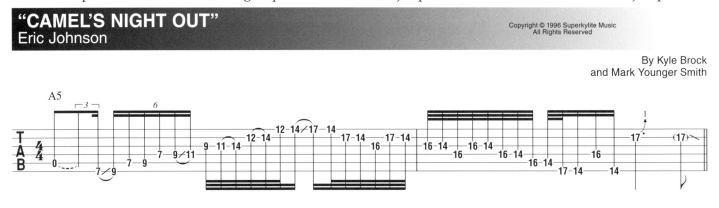

Tapping Sequences

The final sequencing example will use two-handed tapping in the style of Nuno Battencourt, Reb Beach, and Vito Bratta. This pattern uses a six-note sequence in A major incorporating diatonic 3rds and 6ths. One of the advantages of tapping is the ability to easily incorporate larger intervals into a sequence that would normally just contain 2nd and 3rd intervals.

Begin on the sixth string, fret 12 with a right-hand tap and pull off to the fifth fret on the same string a 5th below. Follow that with a hammer-on to the ninth fret, a pull-off back to fret 5, and then two consecutive hammer-ons to the seventh and ninth frets. This pattern is repeated on every other string, altering notes to fit the A major scale.

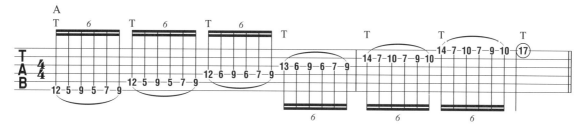

In Nuno Bettencourt's solo on "Get the Funk Out," we see a similar approach to the tapping sequence with some twists and turns. This acrobatic excerpt outlines the chordal structure, emphasizing the roots, 3rds, 5ths, and added 9ths of each chord. Also, notice how the larger one-measure sequence that's played over the B♭ chord is transposed to fit over the C chord, with a little rhythmic displacement. Similarly, the tapping run over the E♭ and F chords in the third and fourth measures are almost identical to each other as transpositions as well.

"GET THE FUNK OUT"
Extreme

Words and Music by Nuno Bettencourt
and Gary Cherone

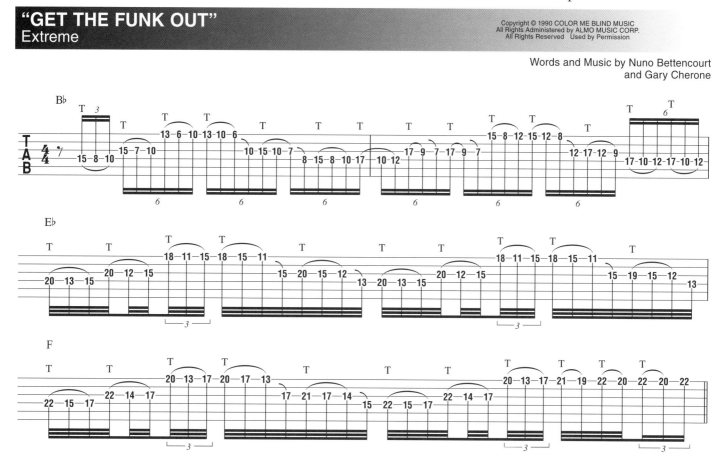

These are some of the most popular sequences used for developing your scale technique, but they're also great to incorporate into your solos. As we've mentioned earlier, too much of a sequence within a solo can cause your solos to become predictable and even sound like practice, so be sure to mix it up! Obviously, the possibilities of creating new sequences are endless. Try to come up with your own patterns and be sure to experiment with new numeric formulas, intervals, and scale types. Also try the sequences we've covered in this chapter, or any you come up with, in all keys, positions, and modes.

LEGATO TECHNIQUE

Many guitarists use the legato technique to create smooth, fluid lines in their solos. While these techniques also facilitate blazing speed, they can also become a distinctive form of expression and dynamics. This chapter is going to look closely at the legato technique, explore some useful exercises, and show you how some of the masters use this technique.

It's interesting how many guitarists don't feel the need to practice legato techniques. Many guitarists know some typical clichéd licks that use some hammer-ons and pull-offs, but not nearly as many players have a real command of the technique. They figure, "If I can pick every note of a lick, then I can surely play it with hammer-ons and pull-offs." This is definitely *not* the case. All three legato techniques should be practiced on scales, modes, arpeggios, and sequences, and incorporated into your solos. First, let's look at the three building blocks of the legato technique.

Hammer-Ons

The *hammer-on* creates an ascending interval by plucking a note, then quickly slamming another finger onto the fretboard above the first note to create the sound of the second note. While this should be done with speed and precision, there is no need to *press* the hammered note any harder than you would to sound any normal note. It's the momentum—not the pressure—that creates the sound. Too much pressure will lead to tension, and, as with all of the techniques introduced in this book, relaxing is critical to proper technique development. Here is an example of what a hammer on looks like when notated.

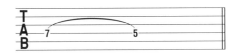

Pull-Offs

You might say that the *pull-off* is the opposite of the hammer-on, except the technique is very different. This time, we are going to create a descending interval by plucking the higher note and creating the sound of the lower note by quickly pulling the finger off of the string. The finger used for the higher note of the pull-off is essentially plucking the string. If you bring your finger directly away from the fretboard, you won't get much of a sound. For the best result, you will need to pull down or up to create a strong tone. Here is an example of what a pull-off looks like in notation.

Slides

To create the *slide*, pluck a note and, while still pressing into the fretboard, move your finger to a different note on the same string. The interval you create can either be ascending or descending, depending on the direction you move. A single slide can be fast or slow and may also include more than one note. Be aware that the faster the slide, the more volume you create, and that a slow slide results in a decrease in volume. Here is an example of what a slide looks like notated.

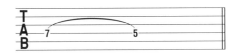

While the above example slides from one note to another, the next example moves through an entire scale. Pluck the C (second string, first fret) and then slide up the C major scale.

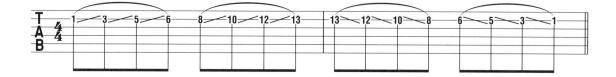

Exercises and Examples

Now that you know the basics of legato playing, you're ready to take this to the next level. We're going to start off with a few exercises for each legato technique that will let you know right away where you stand. Then, we'll look at how some of the masters incorporate it into their solos.

The Old 1–2–3–4

The first exercise is based on the familiar 1–2–3–4 exercises we used earlier in this book, but instead of picking each note, we are going to use the legato technique to create most of the sound. Pick the first note of each string and then use either a hammer-on or a pull-off to sound the other three notes. Again, this is the same as one of our warm-up exercises, but now that you're warmed up (you are, aren't you?), feel free to increase the speed of this one.

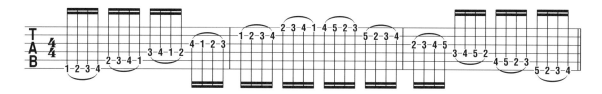

Triplet Version

Our next exercise is the triplet version of the previous exercise, but instead of using your strongest fingers—index, middle, and ring—you're going to use middle, ring, and pinky. Say hello to the burn on this one!

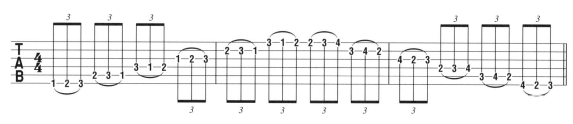

4–3–2–1 Descending

Number 3 is the descending version of our previous 1–2–3–4 exercise. While example 46 is similar, it primarily uses hammer–ons. This exercise uses more pull-offs and will really separate the men from the mice. Make sure you're playing cleanly before increasing the speed!

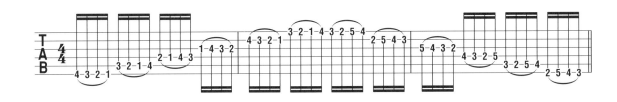

Triplet Version Descending

Next up is the triplet descending version, again using more pull-offs. Remember to use your middle, ring, and pinky fingers for this one.

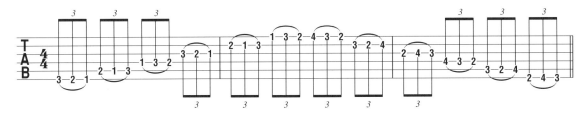

With all four of these exercises, you should continue the pattern all the way up to fret 12. Because these exercises are a serious workout, you should take breaks if you have any pain or feel fatigued. Also, it is very important to use a metronome, especially when practicing hammers and pulls. Not only will it help develop a strong sense of timing, you can chart your progress; make sure you begin with a warm-up speed instead of warp speed!

G Major Scale

A very common application of the legato technique is to play scalar runs using three notes per string. This is a good way to get all four fingers involved in the legato process. Let's start with an ascending G major scale in triplets using all hammer-ons. Pick only once for each new string.

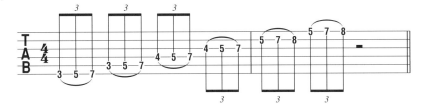

Now, slide up to the next position and come down the scale with pull-offs. Notice that, in order to get back to the beginning of the scale, you'll need to slide back one whole step. Strive for a smooth sound and a consistent volume throughout.

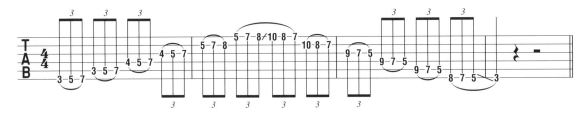

In this example from the Steely Dan classic, "Peg," Jay Graydon uses three notes per string to quickly ascend the G major scale starting at C on the sixth string. Notice the shift on the third string to move into the next position of the scale, enabling the lick to continue the three-note legato climb.

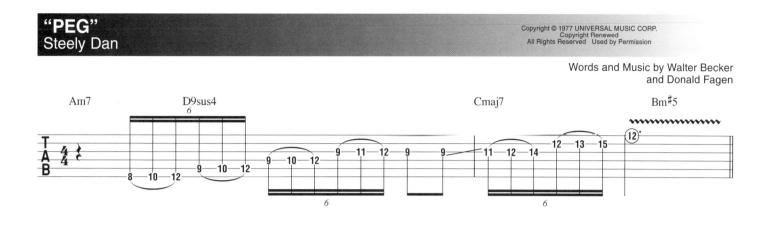

Words and Music by Walter Becker
and Donald Fagen

Placing the Accents

One rut that players tend to get into with legato playing is letting the fingers dictate the rhythms. In other words, if they're playing three notes per string, they always play triplets or sextuplets. If it's two notes per string, it's eighth or sixteenth notes, etc. It's very important to be able to place the accent anywhere in the legato phrase and not just where the picked note falls. This control will free you up to use any rhythm you want.

Three Notes Per String: Sixteenth Notes

Let's start by playing the G major scale with three notes per string, but we'll play it in sixteenth notes instead of triplets. Be sure to accent the first note of each sixteenth for emphasis. You may find this a little harder than it seems, especially at faster tempos, but it's an essential skill to develop.

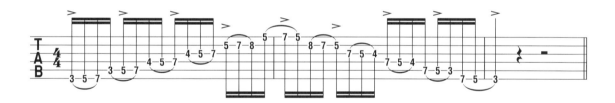

In this excerpt from the great Randy Rhoads on the song "Flying High Again," you can see an example of a descending three-notes-per-string F♯ minor scale pattern using sixteenth notes. Once Rhoads hits the third string, he adds a C♮ from the blues scale, as he does an octave lower on the fifth string. While the second measure accents fall on the beat, notice how the first measure accents are varied.

Words and Music by Ozzy Osbourne,
Randy Rhoads, Bob Daisley
and Lee Kerslake

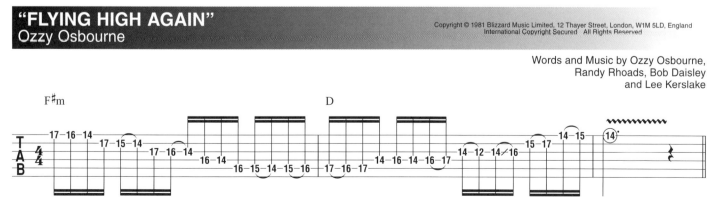

Two Notes Per String: Triplets

Now let's try playing an A minor pentatonic scale with two notes per string using triplets. Remember that this line should feel like triplets, with the accent appearing on each downbeat.

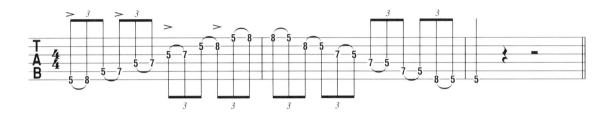

Being able to control the placement of accents with the legato technique is very crucial and should not be neglected. Practice the examples in this chapter until you have the control you need and can really feel the accent where it should be.

Hammer-On from Nowhere

Many times when descending through the strings, players will use the "hammer-on from nowhere" technique for improved speed and uniformity of sound. This works best with a distorted sound.

The concept is pretty simple. When you're moving from one string down to a lower string, you don't have to use the pick. Instead, you can hammer down on the fret with your fretting finger. Let's try this technique with a descending A minor pentatonic scale.

Some players will also use this technique when ascending, but it's more difficult because you have to time the hammer-on with the release of another finger. Let's try this with an ascending A minor pentatonic scale.

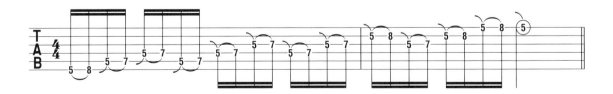

A great example of the hammer-on from nowhere is the endless riff in the AC/DC song "Thunderstruck." Played entirely on the second string, Angus Young uses a B Mixolydian mode. Each note of this sixteenth-note riff is alternated with the open B string. Start slowly and work your way up the lightning speed of this tune.

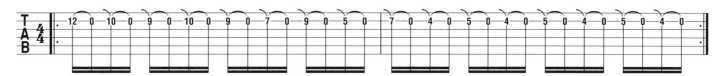

Words and Music by Angus Young
and Malcolm Young

Let's try a few licks that will incorporate this technique. This first one is a nice sixteenth-note descending lick in E minor that repeats an octave lower. Remember, you pick once at the beginning and that's it.

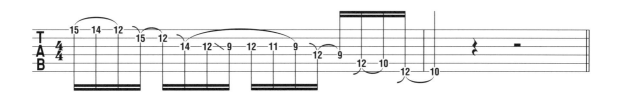

This next one in A minor uses many different rhythms, including sixteenths, sextuplets, and thirty-second notes.

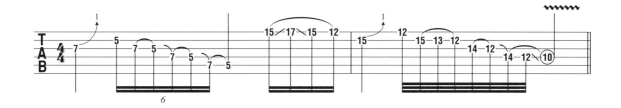

Here's one that mixes A Dorian with the A blues scale.

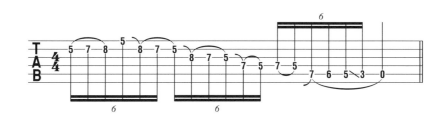

And here's one in D minor that uses several slides to change positions.

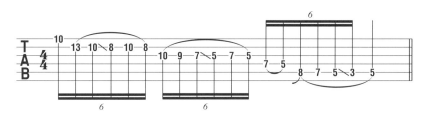

One-String Technique

Another common application of legato is the one-string technique, where you traverse the neck along one string using nothing but hammer-ons, pull-offs, and slides. Hendrix used this technique quite often, as did Stevie Ray Vaughan.

Players like to use this technique with sort of a rhapsodic rhythm, which can create a slithery, sinuous effect. Basically, you choose a scale, choose a string, and then let your fingers do the walking.

Here's a basic example of this idea, applied to a G major pentatonic scale on the G string.

Here's another example of this technique using a G Mixolydian line, also on the G string.

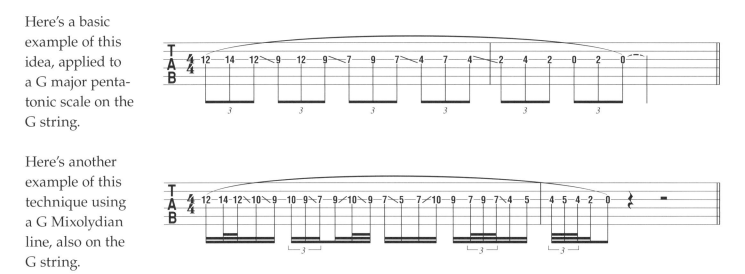

As mentioned before, Stevie Ray Vaughan liked to use this one-string technique in his solos. Below is an excerpt from his beautiful instrumental tune "Lenny." In this example, Vaughan uses a series of hammer-ons, slides, and pull-offs on the second string to begin this classic solo. The notes are right out of the E major pentatonic scale and all played on the second string.

"LENNY"
Stevie Ray Vaughan

Written by Stevie Ray Vaughan

Although some players apply the legato technique only as a means to play as fast as possible, there are many sonic textures possible when these techniques are thought of as a means for creative expression. Experiment and see what you can come up with!